THE
COUPLE'S
GRATITUDE
JOURNAL

5 MINUTES TO CREATE A STRONGER & MORE FULFILLING RELATIONSHIP

SOPHIA GODKIN, PHD

Better Life
BOOKS

Art Director: Kristina Spencer

Editor: Chandi Lyn

Author Photograph Courtesy of Urban Girl Photography, Marcela Bullen

ISBN: 979-8-9877936-0-2

Library of Congress Control Number: 2023903462

To anyone who has ever wanted to
bring a little more love and connection
into their relationship, this one's for you.

Appreciation can make a day — even change a life. Your willingness to put it into words is all that is necessary.

– MARGARET COUSINS

THIS JOURNAL BELONGS TO:

_____

INTRODUCTION

Welcome to *The Couples Gratitude Journal*, your guide to improving your relationship through the power of gratitude. I'm excited to take this journey with you and explore the many ways gratitude can deepen your connection and strengthen your bond with your partner.

Many people ask me how I got started in the art and science of happiness and relationships, and the truth is, it all began with a personal journey of self-growth and development. As an empathetic young girl turned professor and psychologist, I've long been driven by a curiosity of what makes people truly happy in relationships and in life—not just on the surface but deep on the inside.

The older I got, the more aware I became of my own struggles and those of the people closest to me when it came to cultivating happy relationships and a happy life. The more I grew aware of the struggles, the more I wanted to alleviate them. Over the years, my life's work has become a response to that desire. Today, I coach individuals and couples, teach courses, and lead programs to help people cultivate satisfying relationships and become genuinely happy regardless of their past or present circumstances.

It was in my early 20s that I had one of the biggest revelations of my life— it was I who was adding to the dissatisfaction I felt in life.

If I wanted to be happier, I needed to change how I thought, felt, and did things. If I didn't, my mind would continue to habitually focus on the negative in people and things (a survival mechanism each of our minds has) and I would automatically repeat old patterns simply because they were familiar, not because they gave me joy and peace of mind.

Nowhere was this more true than in my relationships. I wanted to build a truly loving relationship, but time after time it became much easier to focus on the not-so-good instead of the good. As a result, my relationships would fizzle and fail. That's when it hit me: **Healthy and happy relationships don't just happen— they need to be cultivated through regular attention and intentional positive actions.**

I began to reach for practical ways to make my relationships feel better and last longer and before long, it became clear that gratitude was a big part of the solution.

Gratitude is a short-term feeling and also a long-term quality of appreciating what we have in life. When times are good, being grateful means celebrating and magnifying the goodness around us so as not to take it for granted. And when times are tough, it means honoring the difficulty and simultaneously looking for hope, healing, and beauty to gain perspective and be less overwhelmed by the pain.

When we're grateful, we're able to acknowledge the goodness in our lives and recognize the real value gratitude adds to our emotional, spiritual, and material well-being. For years, research has shown that grateful people are less stressed, depressed, and lonely. They are also generally more motivated, optimistic, and emotionally resilient. They even have more energy, less pain, and they sleep better too. Small expressions of gratitude have a broad-reaching effect on our own happiness and by connecting us to the best in ourselves and each other, gratitude can even be a key to happiness in our relationships.

Gratitude is all about consciously and intentionally choosing to cultivate thoughts, feelings, and actions that express appreciation, and a gratitude journal is a great way to do it. Investing just a few minutes every day—or whenever you can—to focus your intentions and express the things you're most grateful for will make a big difference in your life.

GRATITUDE IS GOOD FOR RELATIONSHIPS

If you ask most people what they want in their relationships, they'll likely say they want understanding, closeness, connection, support, acceptance, and trust. Incredibly, gratitude plays a crucial role in achieving these very desires.

Consistently grateful couples feel more warmth, intimacy, and satisfaction. They experience more mutual care, support, and stability in their relationships. Couples who feel and express their appreciation as a way of celebrating the positive in each other and their relationship are more empathetic and understanding of one another, and regularly do things that help keep the relationship close. It's no surprise then that couples who practice gratitude together tend to stay together too.

The best part is that gratitude is a skill, choice, and approach to life that you can practice, learn, adopt, and reap the benefits of through the simple practice of journaling. Journaling and sharing what you're grateful for helps focus your attention on positive things that you might otherwise take for granted, and whether you think it's wonderful or cheesy, the fact is, it works.

Whether you're dating, newly married, or been together for many years, by picking up The Couple's Gratitude Journal, you've taken a big step to nourish a relationship that's important to you. All that's left to do now is practice. As English author Frederick Langbridge once said, "we make our habits...and our habits make us." Consider this journal a helpful guide to making a habit out of being grateful. Then watch that gratitude shape your relationship into a happier, closer, and more satisfying one.

Let's dive in.

HOW TO USE THIS JOURNAL

The Couple's Gratitude Journal is your sidekick to transforming your relationship from tension to connection, from full of doubt to full of confidence, and from plain 'ol good to pretty great.

Through the well-established and scientifically-proven practice of writing and sharing what you're grateful for, this journal provides you with a simple and effective way to give your relationship the attention and connection that it needs to truly thrive and flourish. Whether you're looking to improve your relationship or to maintain an already happy one, this journal has got you covered.

Any time is a good time to practice gratitude. Whether it's over the phone during lunch, before dinner, or right before bed, if you and your partner have a few minutes to spare, just open up the journal, fill in the date, and write. Complete one page every night or a page a week. It's up to you. Every little bit counts and this journal is designed to work with you, no matter who you are or how busy your life is. Some couples prefer to share one journal and pass it back and forth, while others prefer to have their own separate journal. Choose the option that works best for you.

Here's what you can expect as you flip the pages and embark on your journey to a stronger relationship.

PROMPTS, QUOTES, AND AFFIRMATIONS

On each page, you will find two prompts. By inviting you to either FIND (notice a new positive quality about your partner you might've previously overlooked) or REMIND (remember what you already love about your partner), each set of prompts helps you reconnect with what's good about your partner to BIND your relationship, making the connection between you a deeper and stronger one.

On each page, you will also find a quote that's intentionally placed to connect you with the wisdom of people whose lives were positively changed by gratitude. At the bottom of each page you'll find an affirmation designed to help you adopt a balanced, positive view of yourself, your partner, and your relationship. I invite you and your partner to each repeat this affirmation out loud or silently to yourself as you visualize and internalize its message.

Keep in mind that throughout the book, I use the word 'partner' to refer to the person you are in a close relationship with and sharing this book with. Any time you see this word, feel free to replace it with any other term that applies to your relationship, such as girlfriend, boyfriend, husband, wife, fiancé, best friend, or significant other. While this journal is designed primarily for romantic couples, it equally benefits a couple of friends, siblings, or just a pair of people looking to grow a closer bond.

FEEL, WRITE, AND SHARE

The key to getting the most out of your gratitude practice is to feel, write, and share. In that order.

FEEL. True gratitude isn't just a list of things you're grateful for; it's a feeling of deep, genuine appreciation that comes from the heart. To feel and express it genuinely, you need to connect with and speak from your heart.

One way to do this is to read the prompt, close your eyes, and take a few deep breaths to quiet any distractions and settle your thoughts. Allow yourself to welcome any thoughts and feelings of what you might be grateful for, no matter how small. No quality, situation, or event is too insignificant to inspire gratitude.

Whatever you do, don't force it. True gratitude comes from emotional honesty—it doesn't ignore your desires, feelings, and needs and it doesn't pretend that everything is perfect. If you're not naturally feeling grateful when you pick up the book, that's okay. Acknowledge how you really feel—whether frustrated, happy, sad, disappointed, excited, etc.—and start there.

WRITE. Once you've read the prompt and connected with a feeling of gratitude inside you, take turns writing your answers (if you're sharing a journal) or write simultaneously in your individual journals.

To inspire yourself to feel deep gratitude, it's helpful to get specific about what you're grateful for. After you've answered the prompt, ask yourself "What about that was good?" and continue writing. The more specific you are, the better.

SHARE. Gratitude is both a personal and a shared experience. After you've each written your answers, take the time to verbally share what you wrote. This may be uncomfortable at first, especially if you're not used to being open and vulnerable with your partner. I encourage you to call on your courage and stay open, as it is through sharing that gratitude turns everyday moments into genuinely positive and connected experiences.

A FINAL NOTE:

Remember, the goal of practicing gratitude is to acknowledge and appreciate the positive aspects of your partner and your relationship that you might
otherwise overlook. The goal isn't to be overly grateful and ignore your
partner's disregard or disrespect. Gratitude is most effective when prac-
ticed in healthy, respectful relationships that have normal ebbs and flows of
satisfaction and dissatisfaction. Relying on gratitude to repair an unhealthy
relationship might lead you to tolerate abuse and disrespect, and to stay in a
relationship that you might otherwise benefit from ending. As such, this journal
serves as a great supplement to, but not a replacement for, therapy or other
forms of professional guidance.

THANK YOU

Thank you for choosing to invest in yourself and your relationship. As a small token of my appreciation, I invite you to explore my complimentary *Guide to Happier and Stronger Relationships*. Inside, you'll find eight practical strategies to help you improve your relationship and deepen your connection with your partner. To access your copy, simply head to www.TheHappinessDoctor.com/guides.

DATE

_____ / _____ / _____

There is always something to be thankful for.

— RHONDA BYRNE

A skill you have that I admire _____

_____

_____

_____

_____

_____

_____

One way you've shown up for me _____

_____

_____

_____

_____

_____

_____

*I'm curious to see what happens if I consciously
take steps to appreciate my partner.*

*It's not what we have in our life, but
who we have in our life that counts.*

– J.M. LAURENCE

Spending time with you is really _____

_____

_____

_____

_____

_____

_____

In you, I have someone with whom I can share _____

_____

_____

_____

_____

_____

_____

My life is better with my partner in it.

Feeling gratitude and not expressing it is like
wrapping a present and not giving it.

– WILLIAM ARTHUR WARD

I can never thank you enough for that time you _____

_____

_____

_____

_____

_____

_____

When I talk about you to people who don't know you, I often say you're

_____

_____

_____

_____

_____

_____

_____

Today I choose to see my partner with grateful eyes.

DATE

_____ / _____ / _____

There is no one like you. I am so glad you exist.

— KIRSTEN ROBINSON

This is an activity I enjoy doing especially with you, and here are a few

reasons why. _____

_____

_____

_____

_____

_____

_____

One thing I love about you that makes you "you", and one reason why

_____

_____

_____

_____

_____

_____

_____

I enjoy seeing my partner smile.

I don't have to chase extraordinary moments to find happiness—it's right in front of me if I'm paying attention and practicing gratitude.

– BRENÉ BROWN

I am grateful that you took the time to help me with _____

_____

_____

_____

_____

_____

_____

The biggest reason you are so important to me _____

_____

_____

_____

_____

_____

_____

*Our gratitude makes all the difference between
simply being together and being happy together.*

DATE

_____ / _____ / _____

The best thing to hold onto in life is each other.

– AUDREY HEPBURN

My favorite place to go with you, and why _____

_____

_____

_____

_____

_____

_____

A moment we shared that I want to replay a hundred times _____

_____

_____

_____

_____

_____

_____

I have patience with myself and my partner.
Building a stronger connection takes time.

DATE

_____ / _____ / _____

When we look for the good in others,
we discover the best in ourselves.

– WILLIAM ARTHUR WARD

You are even more _____ than I first realized,

and I think that's pretty special because _____

_____

_____

_____

_____

_____

_____

I am inspired by how you _____

_____

_____

_____

_____

_____

_____

By lifting my partner up, I lift myself up too.

7

Connecting with those you know love, like and appreciate you restores the spirit and gives you energy to keep moving forward in this life.

– DEBORAH DAY

I treasure many things you do for me, especially _____

_____

_____

_____

_____

_____

_____

One thing I love about your personality, and why _____

_____

_____

_____

_____

_____

_____

I'm happy to give my relationship the effort and attention it deserves.

*Enjoy the little things, for one day you may look
back and realize they were the big things.*

– ROBERT BRAULT

Troubles that I don't have to go through thanks to you _____

_____

_____

_____

_____

_____

_____

I really enjoy spending time _____ with you.

Here are a few reasons why. _____

_____

_____

_____

_____

_____

_____

The little things in my relationship mean a lot to me.

If you want to make a difference in your life—get grateful.

– UNKNOWN

Something I haven't thanked you for that I want to thank you for now

_____

_____

_____

_____

_____

_____

_____

One way you've contributed to making today better than yesterday

_____

_____

_____

_____

_____

_____

_____

*I make it a point to be thankful for everything
about my partner that I once took for granted.*

The most important things to say are those which often I did not think necessary for me to say—because they were too obvious.

– ANDRÉ GIDE

Having you in my life has undoubtedly made me more _____

_____

_____

_____

_____

_____

_____

One reason our relationship is one of the things that matters most to me right

now _____

_____

_____

_____

_____

_____

_____

*It's becoming more natural to find words to
express how I feel about my partner.*

Saying thank you creates love.

– DAPHNE ROSE KINGMA

What I appreciate most about spending days off with you, and a few reasons
why _____

_____

_____

_____

_____

_____

_____

The meal I love sharing with you most, and why _____

_____

_____

_____

_____

_____

_____

*I am gentle and loving towards my partner
as we each learn to appreciate each other
more and love each other better.*

Sometimes the little things in life mean the most.

– ELLEN HOPKINS

This is something I'm proud of you for, and here are a few reasons why.

_____

_____

_____

_____

_____

_____

_____

Whenever you _____, I feel so lucky to be your

partner because _____

_____

_____

_____

_____

_____

_____

Having the partner I want starts with
being the partner I want.

Love those who appreciate you, and appreciate those who love you.

— CONNOR CHALFANT

One reason you're easy to love _____

_____

_____

_____

_____

_____

_____

A quality you see in me that I have trouble seeing in myself _____

_____

_____

_____

_____

_____

_____

*I forgive myself for any time I let my own worries
and busyness shape how I showed up for my partner.*

Know and understand that there will be challenges and difficult times. Don't try to avoid them. Welcome them. Gratefully.

− NEALE DONALD WALSCH

I see the effort you're putting into *this* and I am so proud of you because

_____

_____

_____

_____

_____

_____

_____

Of all the good things you do, *this* is your greatest gift to the world, and why

_____

_____

_____

_____

_____

_____

_____

I turn towards my partner when life gets tough, not away.

DATE

_____ / _____ / _____

The more you thank life, the more life gives you to be thankful for.

– UNKNOWN

A time you showed up for me in the last few months without being asked

_____

_____

_____

_____

_____

_____

_____

A time you put on a brave face when I was scared even though you might've

been scared too _____

_____

_____

_____

_____

_____

_____

The choices I make today shape the
relationship I'm in tomorrow.

When I count my blessings, I count you twice.

— BO LANIER

I appreciate the times you've given me advice—especially that time I came to you for help and you said _____

_____

_____

_____

_____

_____

_____

One way that you've been a good friend to me _____

_____

_____

_____

_____

_____

_____

It is up to me—and only me—to attend to my relationship and not take it for granted.

*I find the most beautiful moments of life aren't just
with you but because of you.*

– LEO CHRISTOPHER

One of the best parts about being in a relationship with you

_____

_____

_____

_____

_____

_____

_____

I wouldn't mind reliving the day we _____

_____

_____

_____

_____

_____

_____

*I find reasons to be satisfied with
my relationship every day.*

DATE

_____ / _____ / _____

Two kinds of gratitude: The sudden kind we feel for what we take; the larger kind we feel for what we give.

– EDWIN ARLINGTON ROBINSON

Something you do regularly that I depend on but often miss the opportunity to thank you for _____

_____

_____

_____

_____

_____

_____

With you, I feel less _____

_____

_____

_____

_____

_____

_____

Focusing on being grateful in the present makes our future better.

*When we focus on our gratitude, the tide of
disappointment goes out and the tide of love rushes in.*

– KRISTIN ARMSTRONG

One good thing that came out of a really hard situation we faced together

_____

_____

_____

_____

_____

_____

_____

You rarely do *this* and I appreciate that so much because _____

_____

_____

_____

_____

_____

_____

*Gratitude is my best defense against
disconnection and conflict in my relationship.*

Thank you. I appreciate you. I love you.

– WALD WASSERMANN

That time you apologized for *this* meant a lot to me. Here's why. _____

_____

_____

_____

_____

_____

_____

We have shared many experiences—not all have been easy. One hard experience we shared that turned out to be a blessing in disguise was when

_____

_____

_____

_____

_____

_____

_____

Love doesn't simply grow and survive on its own;
I maintain it through my words and actions.

*Be with each other. Put away your phone and talk
to each other... Because, we as a human, always take
someone or something for granted.*

– FIY SURI, KALA RUNTUH SELURUHNYA

Something about you that I sometimes take for granted _____

_____

_____

_____

_____

_____

_____

You make us and our relationship a priority when you _____

_____

_____

_____

_____

_____

*Today I practice the feeling of being thankful
for who and what I already have in my life.*

DATE

_____ / _____ / _____

Gratitude is the foundation of all relationships. It's the glue that holds everything together.

– KRISTIN ARMSTRONG

One way that you add fun or joy to my life _____

_____

_____

_____

_____

_____

_____

You were in my corner when you _____

_____

_____

_____

_____

_____

_____

I enjoy the things that already make my relationship a good one.

DATE

_____ / _____ / _____

Never let the things you want make you forget the things you have.

– SANCHITA PANDEY

One reason our relationship is already pretty great _____

_____

_____

_____

_____

_____

_____

When I imagine my life without you, I _____

_____

_____

_____

_____

_____

_____

I appreciate what I have with my partner
as we continue to work on more of what we want.

The heart that gives thanks is a happy one, for we cannot feel thankful and unhappy at the same time.

– DOUGLAS WOOD

It's my job to make me happy but you sure help by _____

_____

_____

_____

_____

_____

_____

Thanks to you, I get to _____

_____

_____

_____

_____

_____

The more grateful I am, the easier it is to be happy in my relationship.

It's not where you are in life, it's who you have by your side that matters.

– UNKNOWN

You totally had my back that one time when _____

_____

_____

_____

_____

_____

_____

We all have bad days. You made my last bad day a little bit better by

_____

_____

_____

_____

_____

_____

_____

My partner and I can do so much more together than we can on our own.

DATE

_____ / _____ / _____

There's nothing nicer than unexpected
appreciation. If you're grateful, get a pen.

– HELEN ELLIS

Your _____ never fails to make me smile. Here's

why. _____

_____

_____

_____

_____

_____

_____

I know, without a doubt, that your past self would be so proud of who you've

become today because _____

_____

_____

_____

_____

_____

_____

My gestures of appreciation make our bond stronger.

DATE

_____ / _____ / _____

Practicing gratitude is like turning the dimmer switch up.
Things you never noticed before keep lighting up your heart.
(They always were there, just unlit.)

— KELLY CORBET

If I changed the time in my life that I spent with you, I wouldn't be

_____

_____

_____

_____

_____

_____

_____

This is one thing that you take off my plate of life. _____

_____

_____

_____

_____

_____

I am proud of the ways I'm learning to
appreciate my relationship more.

At the end of the day, you can either focus on what's tearing you apart or what's holding you together.

– UNKNOWN

I love that we are on the same page about _____

_____

_____

_____

_____

_____

_____

How we handled *this* together showed me that we could get through any-

thing. Here are a few reasons why. _____

_____

_____

_____

_____

_____

_____

Instead of focusing on what in my relationship drains me, today I focus my energy on what sustains me.

We're all a little weird. And life is a little weird. And when we find someone whose weirdness is compatible with ours, we join up with them and fall into mutually satisfying weirdness—and call it love—true love.

— ROBERT FULGHUM

Something about you that's very attractive to me _____

_____

_____

_____

_____

_____

_____

One way that you are my kind of weird _____

_____

_____

_____

_____

_____

_____

I look for the good in my partner and they also look for the good in me.

DATE

_____ / _____ / _____

... don't be so busy "doing you" that you lose sight of those who love and support you... Appreciate the good people in your life when it counts, not when it's convenient.

– LIZ FAUBLAS

One way you've made me feel important _____

_____

_____

_____

_____

_____

_____

A time you handled my heart with the same love and care that you handle

your own _____

_____

_____

_____

_____

_____

_____

Appreciation is how I bring joy into my relationship.

Being told you're appreciated is one of the simplest and most uplifting things you can hear.

— SUE FITZMAURICE

One way that you've helped me to see the good in me _____

_____

_____

_____

_____

_____

_____

What I admire most about you as a person, and a few reasons why

_____

_____

_____

_____

_____

_____

_____

Every time I practice gratitude, I am reminded that who and what I have is enough.

You are the best because you brought out the best in us.

– UNKNOWN

I am thankful you taught me to appreciate *this*. It's been a good lesson

because _____

_____

_____

_____

_____

_____

_____

I probably don't tell you this enough, but one thing I hope you always know

is that _____

_____

_____

_____

_____

_____

_____

*It's not how long we're together, but how
well we love each other that matters most.*

Being appreciated is the strongest encouragement.

– UNKNOWN

I was inspired/encouraged/uplifted when you _____

_____

_____

_____

_____

_____

_____

It's impossible for anyone who knows you not to notice how good you are at

_____

_____

_____

_____

_____

_____

_____

*When life knocks my partner down,
I make it a priority to build him/her/them up.*

A compliment is verbal sunshine.

– ROBERT ORBEN

Sharing a meal with you is always a treat—especially that one time when you

cooked/packed/picked up _____

_____

_____

_____

_____

_____

_____

I hope you never stop being your _____

and _____ self. Here are a few reasons why.

_____

_____

_____

_____

_____

_____

*Today is a new day and a new opportunity to
learn more and love more about my partner.*

Showing gratitude is one of the simplest yet most powerful things humans can do for each other.

— RANDY PAUSCH

A song, movie, book, or art form I love thanks to you _____

_____

_____

_____

_____

_____

_____

Thank you for introducing me to _____.

I'm grateful to know him/her/them because _____

_____

_____

_____

_____

_____

_____

The three most important words in my relationship—I appreciate you.

Let us be grateful to people who make us happy, they are the charming gardeners who make our souls blossom.

– MARCEL PROUST

I like how I feel about myself when I'm around you because _____

_____

_____

_____

_____

_____

_____

I remember when we first started getting to know each other. When I chose to spend more time with you, I knew I was choosing someone who

_____

_____

_____

_____

_____

_____

_____

I'm happy when I see my partner happy.

37

When some things go wrong, take a moment to be thankful for the many more things that are going right.

− ANNIE GOTTLIER

Ups and downs are a part of relationships and a part of life. *This* is one up we've had this year. _____

_____

_____

_____

_____

_____

_____

I'm so thankful for *this* time that you were willing to say "I'm sorry" _____

_____

_____

_____

_____

_____

_____

I know that relationships require regular attention and maintenance, and gratitude is one way I attend to and maintain mine.

Relationships are living things—they require tending.
Like plants, they flourish when they are cared for.

– DAPHNE ROSE KINGMA

A time you lifted me up when I needed it _____

_____

_____

_____

_____

_____

I see the work you put into our relationship, especially when you

_____

_____

_____

_____

_____

_____

Our relationship is what we make it.

To see and to be seen. That is the truest nature of love.

– BRENÉ BROWN

Thank you for making me see *this* truth about myself that I wouldn't have

realized without you. _____

_____

_____

_____

_____

_____

_____

Something you've openly shared about yourself that's made me feel closer to

you _____

_____

_____

_____

_____

_____

_____

Seeing the good in myself helps me
see the good in my partner.

DATE

_____ / _____ / _____

In the end, you need to appreciate things before they are gone.

– SURYA RAJ

A difficult conversation I am glad that we had _____

_____

_____

_____

_____

_____

_____

A valuable lesson that I learned from our latest trouble or challenge

_____

_____

_____

_____

_____

_____

_____

*I can find things to appreciate about my
partner even during tough times.*

*A relationship without gratitude and appreciation
is like a car without fuel. It won't go very far.*

– UNKNOWN

I feel most connected to you when _____

_____

_____

_____

_____

_____

_____

My favorite moment we shared together this year _____

_____

_____

_____

_____

_____

_____

*A bad day in our relationship doesn't mean that we've
failed. Bumps in the road are part of the journey.*

DATE

_____ / _____ / _____

*... a basic law: the more you practice the art of
thankfulness, the more you have to be thankful for.*

– NORMAN VINCENT PEALE

I love that I can rely on you for _____

_____

_____

_____

_____

_____

_____

There is no one else I would rather _____

with. Here are a few reasons why. _____

_____

_____

_____

_____

_____

_____

*Relationships take effort. Today I will make
the effort to show gratitude for my partner.*

To be thankful for one thing is infinitely more powerful than to be bitter about a hundred others.

– CRAIG D. LOUNSBROUGH

A positive change you've made that I appreciate so much _____

_____

_____

_____

_____

_____

_____

Even though I wasn't thankful at the time that you and I went through *this*

challenge, here is one reason I am thankful for it now. _____

_____

_____

_____

_____

_____

_____

*It makes all the difference to appreciate
who and what is in front of me.*

The greatest gift you can give someone is your attention. When
mindfulness embraces those we love, they will bloom like flowers.

– THICH NHAT HANH

One way you have been sensitive to/considerate of my feelings this week

_____

_____

_____

_____

_____

_____

_____

One time you were there for me when I needed you was when

_____

_____

_____

_____

_____

_____

_____

I'm grateful for the opportunity to grow in my relationship.

*When one feels seen and appreciated in their
own essence, one is instantly empowered.*

– WES ANGELOZZI

This is one thing you said or did that let me know that you love and accept

me just the way I am _____

_____

_____

_____

_____

_____

_____

We're all imperfect but *this* is one way you're perfect for me _____

_____

_____

_____

_____

_____

_____

*I don't wait for my partner to become a perfect version
of themselves. I enjoy who they are right now.*

When life is sweet, say thank you and celebrate.
And when life is bitter, say thank you and grow.

– SHAUNA NIEQUIST

A challenge we've gone through that helped me grow _____

_____

_____

_____

_____

_____

_____

One way I've grown as a person this past year thanks in part to you

_____

_____

_____

_____

_____

_____

_____

I am grateful for yesterday's lessons, today's
experiences, and tomorrow's growth.

DATE

_____ / _____ / _____

It's a funny thing about life, once you begin to take
note of the things you are grateful for, you begin
to lose sight of the things that you lack.

— GERMANY KENT

One way that you bring out the best in me, and in us _____

_____

_____

_____

_____

_____

_____

When I'm sad or insecure, you help me by _____

_____

_____

_____

_____

_____

_____

Today I don't assume that my partner
knows I appreciate them—I make sure they know.

Love unspoken weighs heavy on the heart. Give voice to your love.
Love is the only thing in this life with everlasting power.

– JODI LIVON

You are the only person I know who can _____

_____

_____

_____

_____

_____

_____

Hours feel like seconds when we're _____

_____

_____

_____

_____

_____

Today I let go of my bitterness and ingratitude
so that I can find the sweetness in my relationship.
I can't be ungrateful and bitter and expect
my relationship to be sweet.

What a wonderful life I've had. I only wish I'd realized it sooner.

— SIDONIE-GABRIELLE COLETTE

One of our most memorable adventures was when _____

_____

_____

_____

_____

_____

_____

A little thing you did that meant a lot to me, and one reason why

_____

_____

_____

_____

_____

_____

_____

When I replace expectation with appreciation,
I notice that my life is pretty darn good.

*Don't ignore the love you DO have in your life by
focusing on the love you DON'T.*

– MANDY HALE

Without you, I couldn't have _____

_____

_____

_____

_____

_____

_____

Thank you for teaching me _____

_____

_____

_____

_____

_____

*As I focus on how much my partner does for me instead of
what they're not doing, I naturally grow in gratitude.*

It's funny, but have you ever noticed that the more special something is, the more people seem to take it for granted? It's like they think it won't ever change.

– HARVEY WELLINGTON
(NICHOLAS SPARKS—THE WEDDING)

I so enjoyed the last time that we played _____

because _____

_____

_____

_____

_____

If you were gone, I would most miss _____

_____

_____

_____

_____

_____

_____

*I am willing to accept the appreciation
my partner offers me.*

*Let's just be thankful that we get to be on Earth at
the same time as everybody we get to meet.*

– JOMNY SUN

If there was one thing my heart wanted to say to you right now, it would be

_____

_____

_____

_____

_____

_____

_____

One thing about our relationship that I hope never changes, and why

_____

_____

_____

_____

_____

_____

_____

I actively look for opportunities to appreciate my partner.

*The greatest happiness of life is the conviction that we are loved;
loved for ourselves, or rather, loved in spite of ourselves.*

– VICTOR HUGO

This quality of mine isn't always the easiest to be around, but you handle it

like a champ. _____

_____

_____

_____

_____

_____

_____

You make me feel loved when you _____

_____

_____

_____

_____

_____

_____

*May this relationship be a container
where our potential and love can blossom.*

If the world had more people like you it would be
a better place. You do make a difference.

– CATHERINE PULSIFER

If you could see yourself through my eyes, you would know that you are

_____

_____

_____

_____

_____

_____

_____

Two reasons the world needs more people like you _____

_____

_____

_____

_____

_____

_____

Today I seek opportunities to tell my
partner what I love about them.

Go and love someone exactly as they are. And then, watch how they transform into the greatest, truest version of themselves.

– WES ANGELOZZI

One good thing that's happened to me thanks to you _____

_____

_____

_____

_____

_____

_____

My life would be different if we had never met. *This* is one way it would have

been worse without you. _____

_____

_____

_____

_____

_____

I feel thankful for the love in my life right now.

You changed my life without even trying, and I don't think I could ever tell you how much you mean to me. I can't imagine what things would be like if I hadn't met you.

− STEVE MARABOLI

I felt so supported by you this week when _____

_____

_____

_____

_____

_____

_____

A little thing you said or did that made a big difference _____

_____

_____

_____

_____

_____

_____

*I don't hope my way into a great relationship.
I appreciate, care, and love my way
into a great relationship.*

*When we give cheerfully and accept gratefully,
everyone is blessed.*

– MAYA ANGELOU

Something you did for me with no expectation of the favor being returned

_____

_____

_____

_____

_____

_____

_____

An emotional need or desire I have is _____

and *this* is one way you help me to fulfill it _____

_____

_____

_____

_____

_____

_____

I give and receive love in small ways every day.

The moment I spot good in people, they instantly become better.

– RAMESH SOOD

Without you, *this* obstacle would have felt insurmountable. Here are a few

reasons why. _____

_____

_____

_____

_____

_____

_____

Something I accomplished last month with your help that I'm proud of

_____

_____

_____

_____

_____

_____

_____

*My partner and I support our own and
each other's goals and growth.*

When you focus on being the best person you can be, you draw the best possible life, love, and opportunities to you.

– GERMANY KENT

One of the best things about having you in my life is that I get to see you

_____

_____

_____

_____

_____

_____

_____

One way our relationship helps encourage the best version of me

_____

_____

_____

_____

_____

_____

_____

I do my part to create a relationship that feels good.

Life does not have to be perfect to be wonderful.

– ANNETTE FUNICELLO

I really appreciate *this* time that you said yes. It really mattered to me

because _____

_____

_____

_____

_____

_____

_____

Just in case no one has told you lately, you are extremely and totally

_____

_____

_____

_____

_____

_____

_____

*Appreciating my partner is at the top
of my to-do list every day.*

You changed my life without even trying, and I don't think I could ever tell you how much you mean to me. I can't imagine what things would be like if I hadn't met you.

— STEVE MARABOLI

Something I didn't have when you weren't in my life that I am grateful to have

today _____

_____

_____

_____

_____

_____

_____

One way you make my life easier _____

_____

_____

_____

_____

_____

Having my partner by my side makes life more interesting and meaningful.

*Don't forget, a person's greatest emotional need is
to feel appreciated.*

– H. JACKSON BROWN JR.

An unforgettable memory I treasure with you, and why _____

_____

_____

_____

_____

_____

_____

Why focus on what we don't have, when we can focus on all that we do

have, like _____

_____

_____

_____

_____

_____

_____

*I don't need a perfect relationship
to have a happy relationship.*

*Don't let the sun go down without saying thank
you to someone, and without admitting to yourself
that absolutely no one gets this far alone.*

– STEPHEN KING

A good habit you have that I'm thankful I've started to adopt too _____

_____

_____

_____

_____

_____

_____

A time you supported and encouraged my decision _____

_____

_____

_____

_____

_____

*With my appreciation and support, I help my partner
become the best version of themselves.*

When we love, we always strive to become better than we are.
When we strive to become better than we are, everything around
us becomes better too.

– PAULO COELHO

Some people say your best quality is _____,

but I say it's _____ because _____

_____

_____

_____

_____

_____

One way you make me a better person _____

_____

_____

_____

_____

_____

_____

I choose to honor and appreciate my
partner's beauty, strength, and uniqueness.

*Even if some moments are rocky, what matters
most is that you soften and open, and that you
learn from your pain. That's how we heal.*

– HELEN S. ROSENAU

Thank you for putting up with my _____.

I've noticed and I'm truly thankful because _____

_____

_____

_____

_____

_____

_____

Something I've discovered about myself thanks to you _____

_____

_____

_____

_____

_____

_____

*I use challenges in my relationship
to motivate myself to learn and grow.*

*How lucky am I to have something that makes
saying goodbye so hard.*

– WINNIE THE POOH (A.A. MILNE)

If we are in each other's lives for a reason, I think it might be _____

_____

_____

_____

_____

_____

_____

One reason I am afraid to lose you _____

_____

_____

_____

_____

_____

_____

*Every day may not be perfect in our relationship
but there is something perfect in every day.*

*When you stop expecting people to be perfect,
you can like them for who they are.*

– DONALD MILLER

I don't know that anyone will ever be able to match your enthusiasm for

_____

_____

_____

_____

_____

_____

_____

Something about you that's worth celebrating, and one reason why

_____

_____

_____

_____

_____

_____

_____

I happily give and receive love every day.

_To make a difference in someone's life, you don't have to be
brilliant, rich, beautiful, or perfect. You just have to care._

– MANDY HALE

One reason I am attracted to the person you are becoming _____

_____

_____

_____

_____

_____

_____

When you said you would do _this_ and you followed through, it meant a lot to

me because _____

_____

_____

_____

_____

_____

_____

_It's the small moments, like remembering to be grateful,
that make the bigger picture of my relationship._

*Love doesn't just sit there, like a stone, it has to be
made, like bread; remade all the time, made new.*

– URSULA K. LE GUIN

One way you've challenged me to be a better person _____

_____

_____

_____

_____

_____

_____

This was a time when you took responsibility and admitted to being wrong,

and I appreciated it because _____

_____

_____

_____

_____

_____

_____

*The effort I put into creating a healthy,
happy relationship is worth it.*

Love is not only something you feel, it is something you do.

— DAVID WILKERSON

You take an interest in *this* because I'm interested in it, and I am thankful for

that because _____

_____

_____

_____

_____

_____

_____

You've been there for the good times, and also for the bad times. *This* bad

time was particularly rough and I couldn't have made it through without you.

_____

_____

_____

_____

_____

_____

_____

I nurture my relationship with love and care.

*We don't need more to be thankful for, we just
need to be more thankful.*

– CARLOS CASTANEDA

When I see your face or hear your voice, I often feel _____

_____

_____

_____

_____

_____

_____

This is one of my favorite things to do with you. If the last time we did that was

the last time ever, I would feel _____

_____

_____

_____

_____

_____

_____

*Appreciation is my ticket to a happy
relationship. All I need to do is pay attention
and look for opportunities to practice it.*

DATE

_____ / _____ / _____

Gratitude is the memory of the heart.

– JEAN-BAPTISTE MASSIEU

Thanks so much for helping me with *this*. It makes a difference to me because

_____

_____

_____

_____

_____

_____

_____

If there was a formula for what makes you so wonderfully you, it would be

made of these three ingredients _____

_____

_____

_____

_____

_____

_____

*It's with gratitude that my relationship
blossoms into what it's meant to be.*

Invite your heart to be grateful and your thank yous will be heard even when you don't use words.

– PAVITHRA MEHTA

Sometimes I wish you could see yourself the way I see you, full of

_____ and _____

because _____

_____

_____

_____

_____

_____

If anyone can make me feel _____, it's you

because _____

_____

_____

_____

_____

_____

Love is a two-way street that I nurture with gratitude.

You cannot find beauty unless you appreciate beauty. You cannot find friendship unless you appreciate others. You cannot find love unless you appreciate loving and being loved. If you wish abundance, appreciate life.

– WILLIAM R. MILLER

One place I am grateful that we visited together, and why _____

_____

_____

_____

_____

_____

_____

If our relationship was a good news headline, it would read something like

_____

_____

_____

_____

_____

_____

_____

I choose to fill my relationship with thankfulness and joy.

Love and kindness are never wasted. They always make a difference. They bless the one who receives them, and they bless you, the giver.

— BARBARA DE ANGELIS

An act of kindness you've shown me _____

_____

_____

_____

_____

_____

_____

One thing about you that makes you absolutely irreplaceable _____

_____

_____

_____

_____

_____

_____

I find joy in reminding my partner of the good things I see in him/her/them.

Behavior we celebrate grows ever stronger.

– M.J. RYAN

I felt supported in my desire to become a better person this last year when

you _____

_____

_____

_____

_____

_____

_____

The way you see things sometimes helps me see things in a new way. I espe-

cially love your perspective on _____

because _____

_____

_____

_____

_____

_____

_There is so much about being with
my partner that I enjoy._

*In ordinary life we hardly realize that we receive
a great deal more than we give, and that it is only
with gratitude that life becomes rich.*

– DIETRICH BONHOEFFER

Thank you for being there with me when I felt _____

_____

_____

_____

_____

_____

_____

One way I feel safe/secure/comfortable when you're around

_____

_____

_____

_____

_____

_____

_____

*Today I make my partner's feelings
one of my top priorities.*

Everything that I have becomes invisible in my search for everything that I don't have. And when that happens, what I don't have starts to look like the only thing that I do have.

– CRAIG D. LOUNSBROUGH

One way you've made me feel wanted recently _____

_____

_____

_____

_____

_____

_____

One way we're different that's actually a strength and not a barrier, and one

reason why _____

_____

_____

_____

_____

_____

_____

Instead of focusing on the flaws and negatives, today I turn my attention to what I appreciate and enjoy.

*Always be thankful for what you have, because
you never know when it might be gone.*

— MICALEA SMELTZER

One thing in our present that I hope makes its way into our future, and why

_____

_____

_____

_____

_____

_____

_____

Nobody's perfect but it's your willingness to do *this* that brings you pretty

close. _____

_____

_____

_____

_____

_____

_____

Every day I appreciate my partner more and more.

Be good to the people in your life that are too good to replace.

– UNKNOWN

Whether or not you let yourself see it or believe it, you are truly

_____, and here's why _____

_____

_____

_____

_____

I haven't forgotten *this* time that you reminded me of what I am capable of.

_____

_____

_____

_____

_____

_____

_____

I am learning to notice what my partner
does more than what they don't.

DATE

_____ / _____ / _____

Gratitude is the key to a happy relationship. If you want to feel more love, give more love. If you want to feel more appreciation, give more appreciation.

– UNKNOWN

I admire how _____ you are and here is one reason

why. _____

_____

_____

_____

_____

_____

_____

I am so proud of us for _____

_____

_____

_____

_____

_____

_____

I love how my partner's strengths balance my weaknesses.

*Be the reason someone smiles. Be the reason
someone feels loved.*

– ROY T. BENNETT

A strength of yours that I appreciate, and why _____

_____

_____

_____

_____

_____

_____

A fear you've helped me temper or let go of _____

_____

_____

_____

_____

_____

_____

*When I want to feel appreciated, I focus on appreciating
more. That's why one of the best things I can do in my
relationship is to appreciate my partner more.*

*Develop an attitude of gratitude. Say thank you to
everyone you meet for everything they do for you.*

– BRIAN TRACY

A simple pleasure we enjoy together _____

_____

_____

_____

_____

_____

_____

One way you've supported my dreams _____

_____

_____

_____

_____

_____

_____

*I make a conscious effort to think about
my partner's needs and wants.*

Gratitude is the healthiest of all human emotions. The more you express gratitude for what you have, the more likely you will have even more to express gratitude for.

– ZIG ZIGLAR

One way you've been responsive to my needs this week _____

_____

_____

_____

_____

_____

_____

A physical need or desire I have is _____

and one way you help me to satisfy it is by _____

_____

_____

_____

_____

_____

_____

I invest in my relationship every time I show appreciation.

You have a place in my heart no one else ever could have.

– F. SCOTT FITZGERALD

One way you changed my life for the better _____

_____

_____

_____

_____

_____

_____

You are the only one who makes me feel _____

and I think it's because _____

_____

_____

_____

_____

_____

_____

My relationship isn't good because of the love
we shared in the beginning; it's good because
of how well we continue building love every day.

*A thankful heart enjoys blessings twice —when
they're received, and when they're remembered.*

– UNKNOWN

Something you do that I find comfort in, and why _____

_____

_____

_____

_____

_____

_____

Thanks in part to you, *this* is one way that I am a better me mentally, emotion-

ally, physically, and/or spiritually _____

_____

_____

_____

_____

_____

_____

*If I wait for my relationship to be perfect,
I'll miss all of the best parts.*

We do not need to lose people or things to appreciate them.

– MOKOKOMA MOKHONOANA

Through the mountains and valleys of our relationship, I've learned that

_____

_____

_____

_____

_____

_____

_____

One way we're already living the life we once only dreamt of

_____

_____

_____

_____

_____

_____

_____

*What is coming in our relationship
is better than what's gone.*

You could've had anyone in the world, but you chose me. Thank you.

– ANTHONY T. HINCKS

One reason I'm grateful that you chose me as your partner/friend/etc.

_____

_____

_____

_____

_____

_____

_____

I remain committed to our relationship, and here are a few reasons why.

_____

_____

_____

_____

_____

_____

_____

I feel closer to my partner every day.

As we express our gratitude, we must never forget that the highest appreciation is not to utter words, but to live by them.

– JOHN F. KENNEDY

You've been there for the good times, and also for the bad times. *This* bad time was particularly rough and I couldn't have made it through without you.

_____

_____

_____

_____

_____

_____

_____

Thank you for forgiving me for _____.

It meant the world to me because _____

_____

_____

_____

_____

I am grateful for how loved and appreciated I am.

At times our own light goes out and is rekindled by a spark from another person. Each of us has cause to think with deep gratitude of those who have lighted the flame within us.

– ALBERT SCHWEITZER

One way you show respect for me _____

_____

_____

_____

_____

_____

_____

If I were to write you a short love letter right now, here's what it would say

_____

_____

_____

_____

_____

_____

I embrace our relationship through all its phases.

DATE

_____ / _____ / _____

Appreciate the one who appreciates your presence.
Embrace the one who embraces your uniqueness.
Never let go of the one who never let you go.

— ONUR TASKIRAN

My favorite season to spend with you is_____

because _____

_____

_____

_____

_____

_____

If someone asked me to describe you in just three words, I would say

_____

_____

_____

_____

_____

_____

_____

Appreciating the people, experiences, and things in my life
is becoming a normal part of my every day.

It's not happiness that brings us gratitude. It's gratitude that brings us happiness.

– UNKNOWN

A similarity we have that I really appreciate, and one reason why

_____

_____

_____

_____

_____

_____

_____

I'm so glad that despite facing some rough times, we persevered and didn't

throw in the towel because _____

_____

_____

_____

_____

_____

_____

I am continuously learning how to love my partner better.

DATE

_____ / _____ / _____

Celebrate the people in your life who are there because they love you for no other reason than because you are YOU.

– MANDY HALE

A tradition we created and kept up that I enjoy, and a few reasons why

_____

_____

_____

_____

_____

_____

_____

One way that you are proactive in maintaining our connection _____

_____

_____

_____

_____

_____

_____

*Appreciating and being appreciated
feels really good to me.*

Smile every chance you get; not because life has been easy, perfect, or exactly as you had anticipated, but because you choose to be happy and grateful for all the good things you do have and all the problems you know you don't have.

– UNKNOWN

You allowed me to be myself, even with my flaws, when you _____

_____

_____

_____

_____

_____

_____

My world is better with you in it because _____

_____

_____

_____

_____

_____

_____

When I stop expecting my partner to be perfect, I can appreciate him/her/them for who they really are.

When eating fruit, remember the one who planted the tree.

− VIETNAMESE PROVERB

No one makes it through life's difficult transitions on their own, and I can't thank you enough for being there for *this* transition of mine.

_____

_____

_____

_____

_____

_____

_____

One thing that comes easy to us, and why _____

_____

_____

_____

_____

_____

I advocate for our love every time I focus
on my partner's strengths instead of flaws.

DATE

_____ / _____ / _____

Gratitude is a quality similar to electricity: It must be produced and discharged and used up in order to exist at all.

– WILLIAM FAULKNER

A memory we shared that makes me laugh _____

_____

_____

_____

_____

_____

_____

I wish I could _____ like you can because

_____

_____

_____

_____

_____

_____

I do my best to bring closeness where there was once distance and appreciation where there used to be criticism.

Too often we underestimate the power of a touch, a smile, a kind word, a listening ear, an honest compliment, or the smallest act of caring, all of which have the potential to turn a life around.

— LEO BUSCAGLIA

It makes me smile when you _____

_____

_____

_____

_____

_____

_____

A topic or issue that's important to me that you really understand my perspective on _____

_____

_____

_____

_____

_____

_____

I celebrate the moments of joy and laughter shared with my partner.

*Appreciate what you have, where you are, and
who you are with in this moment.*

– TONY CLARK

The happiest day in our relationship so far, and why _____

_____

_____

_____

_____

_____

_____

If I was talking to my younger self, I would tell him/her/them that you've

been a positive presence in my life because _____

_____

_____

_____

_____

_____

_____

*I accept that I am imperfect, and forgive
myself for any moments where I didn't show
up as my best self for my partner.*

The greatest gift you can give someone is your gratitude.
When they know they are appreciated, they will go
to the ends of the earth to help you.

– UNKNOWN

My favorite thing to do with you on our days off is_____

because _____

_____

_____

_____

_____

_____

_____

I miss you when you're not around because _____

_____

_____

_____

_____

_____

_____

With gratitude, I nurture the connection
that my partner and I share.

DATE

_____ / _____ / _____

Silent gratitude isn't much use to anyone.

– GERTRUDE STEIN

When I take you in with all of my senses (i.e., touch, smell, sight, hearing,

taste), I appreciate _____

_____

_____

_____

_____

_____

_____

This is something I didn't know before I met you. _____

_____

_____

_____

_____

_____

_____

*I make it a priority to seek and
speak the good in my partner.*

You need to be aware of what others are doing, applaud their efforts, acknowledge their successes, and encourage them in their pursuits. When we all help one another, everybody wins.

— JIM STOVALL

We have so many great memories together, like _____

_____

_____

_____

_____

_____

_____

One reason I'm excited to share the future with you _____

_____

_____

_____

_____

_____

_____

*I appreciate my partner even as
we work on improving things.*

*Always remember people who have helped you
along the way, and don't forget to lift someone up.*

– ROY T. BENNETT

The world would be a better place if there were more people like you

because _____

_____

_____

_____

_____

_____

_____

One time you helped me weather and not drown from life's storms

_____

_____

_____

_____

_____

_____

_____

I am generous with my love for my partner.

Treat people as if they were what they ought to be and you help them to become what they are capable of being.

— JOHANN WOLFGANG VON GOETHE

I'm quite confident that you are the most _____

person I know because _____

_____

_____

_____

_____

_____

I'm proud of the father/mother/daughter/son/person/etc. you are

because _____

_____

_____

_____

_____

_____

_____

I speak life into my partner every time
I appreciate him/her/them.

Feeling grateful or appreciative of someone or something in your life actually attracts more of the things that you appreciate and value into your life.

– CHRISTIANE NORTHRUP

Something in my home I'm grateful for that you helped put there

_____

_____

_____

_____

_____

_____

_____

If someone asked me, "Why him/her/them?", I'd say _____

_____

_____

_____

_____

_____

_____

Happy in my relationship is a precursor to happy in life. I can't have one without the other.

Happiness is achieved when you stop waiting for your life to begin and start making the most of the moment you are in.

– GERMANY KENT

Even though it might not have turned out perfectly, I am so thankful for the

effort you put into _____

_____

_____

_____

_____

_____

If I could give you an award, it would read "the most_____

person ever." Here are a few reasons why. _____

_____

_____

_____

_____

*Today I bring an open mind and
open heart to my relationship.*

Make it a habit to tell people, 'thank you.' To express your appreciation sincerely and without the expectation of anything in return. Truly appreciate those around you, and you'll soon find many others around you.

– RALPH MARSTON

The quality in you that I'm most attracted to _____

_____

_____

_____

_____

_____

_____

We have the most fun when we _____

_____

_____

_____

_____

_____

_____

I don't have to chase happiness in my relationship, I just need to choose it.

*We must find time to stop and thank the people
who make a difference in our lives.*

– JOHN F. KENNEDY

With you by my side, I can do anything, like _____

_____

_____

_____

_____

_____

_____

This day/month/year was a hard one, but it was easier with you by my side

because _____

_____

_____

_____

_____

_____

_____

*I feel a sense of security and strength
knowing that my partner is by my side.*

Gratitude unlocks the fullness of life. It turns what we have into enough, and more. It turns denial into acceptance, chaos to order, confusion to clarity. It can turn a meal into a feast, a house into a home, a stranger into a friend.

– MELODY BEATTIE

Has anyone ever told you that you have the best _____?

Here's why I think so. _____

_____

_____

_____

_____

_____

Something I always wanted to do that I got to do with you _____

_____

_____

_____

_____

_____

_____

I help us create a stronger relationship by doing the right things, not by doing everything right.

DATE

_____ / _____ / _____

We can only be said to be alive in those moments
when our hearts are conscious of our treasures.

– THORNTON WILDER

You are extremely _____ and that's one quality that
is hard to find. I really appreciate this about you because _____

_____

_____

_____

_____

_____

_____

One reason I'd pick you all over again _____

_____

_____

_____

_____

_____

_____

I am proud of the effort we've put in and
the progress we've made in our relationship.

_The deepest principle in human nature is the
craving to be appreciated._

– WILLIAM JAMES

When I look at you, my eyes often like to land on your _____

_____

_____

_____

_____

_____

_____

I admire your view on _____,

and here are a few reasons why. _____

_____

_____

_____

_____

_____

_____

_Appreciating my partner helps me
to judge less and love more._

DATE

_____ / _____ / _____

Be kind. Be thoughtful. Be genuine. But most of all, be thankful.

– UNKNOWN

Something you do without even trying that amazes me, and one reason why

_____

_____

_____

_____

_____

_____

_____

I'm glad we share values like _____ and

_____ (e.g., trust, loyalty, family, self-development).

They create a good foundation for our relationship because _____

_____

_____

_____

_____

_____

I don't know what's coming
but I like where we are right now.

*Appreciation has tremendous power. A beautiful
thing is not beautiful until someone appreciates it.*

— DEBASISH MRIDHA

The best moment of our relationship was when _____

_____

_____

_____

_____

_____

_____

My favorite part about spending the holidays with you _____

_____

_____

_____

_____

_____

_____

*Gratitude opens my eyes to the small
yet significant moments in our relationship,
making them even more beautiful.*

*...the way to develop the best that is in a person is
by appreciation and encouragement.*

– CHARLES SCHWAB

The best gift I've received from you, and one reason why _____

_____

_____

_____

_____

_____

_____

An important decision that I'm glad we made together, and why

_____

_____

_____

_____

_____

_____

_____

*It doesn't make me a bad partner if I forget to
be grateful sometimes. I just keep trying every day.*

DATE

_____ / _____ / _____

We often take for granted the very things that most deserve our gratitude.

– CYNTHIA OZICK

Our time together is precious and often feels limited. I treasure the moments you share your time with me because _____

_____

_____

_____

_____

_____

_____

One of my favorite things we've done together that I'd love if we did again soon _____

_____

_____

_____

_____

_____

Having a teammate in life makes things easier.

_Gratitude is one of the most powerful human
emotions. Once expressed, it changes attitude,
brightens outlook, and broadens our perspective._

– GERMANY KENT

One time you were my best cheerleader _____

_____

_____

_____

_____

_____

_____

If I could give you a gold medal, it would be for _____

_____

_____

_____

_____

_____

_____

_I welcome the chance to learn, take risks, and
make and correct mistakes in my relationship._

To be fully seen by somebody, then, and be loved anyhow - this is a human offering that can border on miraculous.

– ELIZABETH GILBERT

I look forward to the time we get to spend together because _____

_____

_____

_____

_____

_____

_____

Thank you for valuing me even in my imperfection. *This* is a mistake that you've forgiven me for. _____

_____

_____

_____

_____

_____

_____

*Building my partner up is one way
that I love him/her/them.*

*Respecting, understanding, and appreciating
people makes us better people.*

– CATHY BURNHAM MARTIN

I respect how you _____

_____

_____

_____

_____

_____

_____

A difference between us that I appreciate and respect, and one reason why

_____

_____

_____

_____

_____

_____

_____

*No matter what my relationship looked
like today, there is beauty in it.*

When you take things for granted, you diminish their importance and may even jeopardize their very existence.

– FRANK SONNENBERG

Everyone deserves to be treated well. *This* is how I want to treat you better, and why. _____

_____

_____

_____

_____

_____

One thing in our future that I can't wait to experience, and why

_____

_____

_____

_____

_____

_____

I am fully worthy of a caring and affectionate love.

*Be in a state of gratitude for everything that shows up in your life.
Be thankful for the storms as well as the smooth sailing.*

– WAYNE DYER

A difficulty we experienced that contained a hidden blessing was when

_____

_____

_____

_____

_____

_____

_____

Sure, we've had some ups and downs but in the end _____

_____

_____

_____

_____

_____

_____

*In my relationship, I move with a hope for
progress, not with an expectation of perfection.*

CONTINUE YOUR JOURNEY TO A HAPPIER AND STRONGER RELATIONSHIP

I hope this book has been a helpful guide on your journey to a happier, closer, and more satisfying relationship. To continue your progress, I invite you to read my complimentary *Guide to Happier and Stronger Relationships*, featuring 8 practical strategies to immediately improve your relationship. You can access it at www.TheHappinessDoctor.com/guides.

This is not a goodbye, my darling, this is a thank you. Thank you for coming into my life and giving me joy, thank you for loving me and receiving my love in return. Thank you for the memories I will cherish forever.

— NICHOLAS SPARKS

ACKNOWLEDGMENTS

A big dose of gratitude goes to each of you who said, "the next book you write should be a gratitude journal for couples." I wholeheartedly listened.

To Tieg Alexander, I can't thank you enough for being my rock as I grew into the type of person capable of creating and maintaining loving and fulfilling relationships.

To Cory Meisenheimer, thank you for sharing your entrepreneurial spirit with me and giving me the motivation to turn this book into a reality.

And to Oleg Bershadsky, thank you for the encouragement that made it possible for me to bring this book to life in a way that truly reflects my vision.

ABOUT THE AUTHOR

Psychologist and Happiness & Relationship Coach turned best-selling author **SOPHIA GODKIN, PHD** inspires people around the world to trade in superficial and fleeting happiness for true happiness from the inside out. Her practical tools to help people effectively work through and heal their emotions, relationships, and past experiences benefit many through her individual coaching, courses, and coaching programs, both online and in person.

As a renowned coach, university professor, and head of learning at national and international wellness companies, Dr. Sophia has coached people around the world in the art of happiness, relationships, and emotional healing for 15 years. Her work blends the principles and practice of Positive Psychology with therapeutic approaches like Internal Family Systems Therapy (IFS) to make possible a truly holistic, inclusive, and deeply compassionate pathway to happiness. Dr. Sophia's first book, The 5-Minute Gratitude Journal: Give Thanks, Practice Positivity, Find Joy was released in August 2020 and has sold over 150,000 copies and garnered over 3,000 five-star reviews. Whether in the form of coaching, writing, or group programs, Dr. Sophia is known for the depth, light-heartedness, and transformative potential of her work.

When not busy inspiring and helping people to create a healthier, happier life, Dr. Sophia loves walking or biking along the river, camping and hiking in the local mountains and hills, Salsa and Bachata dancing, practicing yoga, paddling in Idaho's beautiful ponds and lakes, nourishing her emotional and intellectual self through reading, music and reflective practices, and enjoying each moment of being alive in the company of the amazing people she calls friends.

Visit Dr. Sophia online at www.TheHappinessDoctor.com and find her on Instagram @thehappinessdoctor.

www.ingramcontent.com/pod-product-compliance
Lightning Source LLC
Chambersburg PA
CBHW050448150626
46551CB00029B/1989